To CATHY
HOPE YOU ENJOY
THE BOOK AND THE
HOLIDAYS!

"Take all of this book upon reason that you can and the balance on faith, and you will live and die a happier and better man."

—Abraham Lincoln

Mark
Duffield

The Last Shepard & Tales of the Tenth Ornament
A Wee Yarn of Wonder at Christmastime
Published by:
Three Bean Press, LLC
P.O. Box 301711
Jamaica Plain, MA 02130
orders@threebeanpress.com • www.threebeanpress.com

Publishers Cataloging-in-Publication Data
Duffield, Mark
The Last Shepard & Tales of the Tenth Ornament / by Mark Duffield.
p. cm.
Summary: When a Boston gift shop is scheduled to be demolished on Christmas Eve, and its owner is found dead, a young and cynical reporter is sent to cover the story. What he uncovers on that mystical day turns out to be a much bigger story than he anticipated. This is a tale of faith and faith rewarded.
ISBN 978-0-9767276-6-8
[1. Christmas—Fiction. 2. Beliefs—Fiction. 3. Faith—Fiction. 4. Boston—Fiction. 5. Holiday—Fiction.]
I. Sherwood, Don, Ill. II. Duffield, Sharon, Ill. III. Title.

LCCN 2011927009

Typeset in Cochin

Printed and bound in Guangzhou, China, by Everbest Printing Company, Ltd., through Four Colour Print Group in May, 2011. Batch 100535.2

10 9 8 7 6 5 4 3 2 1

The Last Shepard
& Tales of the Tenth Ornament

by Mark Duffield

A Wee Yarn of Wonder at Christmastime
Illustrated by Don Sherwood
with Sharon Duffield

three
bean press

Written for the 100 families of Blackstone's Christmas Mystery Ornament Program

Dedicated to Mom and Dad,
my brothers and sisters: Jim and Hugh, Nancy, Lynn and Sharon,
and my nieces and nephews:
Sharon, Erin, Nancy, Laura and Allyson, Sebastien, Jimmy, Mark, Sean and Scott

{ **In Memory of**
Don Sherwood }

A portion of the proceeds from the sale of the first edition of *The Last Shepard
& Tales of the Tenth Ornament* will benefit pediatric cancer research and care
at MassGeneral Hospital *for* Children (MGH*f*C) Cancer Center.

Preface

I was brought up in a time when oral tradition reigned. Storytelling was a passion and a rite of passage in my family. Tales tall and small, real and imagined, poignant and pensive, historical—and often hysterical—were told and retold 'round the fireplace and dining room table. The fables that unfolded, whether original or passed down, were always peppered with wisdom, wit and self-deprecation. My father and both of my brothers were masters of the spoken word—entertaining raconteurs of the highest order. But it was at Christmastime, when all were gathered from the four winds and the seven seas, that storytelling became high art, competitive and raucous. When unwrapped and revealed, these stories rivaled any gift found under the tree or in our stockings.

My entire world, in fact, was engulfed in the art of storytelling. In the neighborhood of my youth, there were story-telling families everywhere, from the top of the hill to the bottom. For 25 years, our families would gather around a small pond on Christmas Eve to sing carols, exchange gifts and enchant one another with stories. Those families were: Strachan, Rossik, Hobby, Wetzel, De Roeck, Bartoe, Duffield, Johnson, Loh, Wensley, Robinson, Moore, Latham, Blackman, Chudy, Hobbs, Thomas, Marshall, Allard and Cacavelo, Fry, Bryant, Parvin, Sullivan, Potts, Demarest, Williams, Stoeckle, Seaman, Earl, Viarengo, Thomas, Larsen, Miller and Walton. I have wonderful memories of those times and the extraordinary people I grew up with. What fertile ground for the imagination! If we are indeed, to cite Tennyson, a part of all we have seen, then the little tale of *The Last Shepard* is inspired in part by all those I have been fortunate to meet. Therefore, I had much to draw from when spinning this yarn.

To some, perhaps, Christmas might be a battered, worn or somewhat diminished version of what it once was. Why, within some subcultures of American society, even a traditional "Merry Christmas" greeting could be construed as a glaring social faux-pas. But what has been broken down can be restored. This tale, although a Christmas story, is a reflection of the values that are the very essence of Christmas. For the holiday spirit is alive within each of us and expressed uniquely through the stories of our lives. This yarn is woven with the belief that Christmas is to be what is best for you and your family. *The Last Shepard* is a manifestation of hope, meant to inspire good in readers for generations to come.

Chapter 1

You can believe what you please. Your beliefs are none of my business. And mine none of yours. I can only describe for you what I saw—what I experienced—that one snowy Christmas Eve so many years ago.

Please come on in. The snow outside is starting to pick up. Pull up a chair next to the fire. Cider? I have spirits a little stronger. You may need it. I know I do from time to time. Okay, okay, as you wish.

Well, let's see. Where to begin? It was my first assignment as a young reporter for *The Examiner*. I was dispatched to 46 Charles Street on Boston's Beacon Hill to cover the demolition of a small store and the untimely passing of its owner. As you can imagine, I was a bit annoyed about having to work on Christmas Eve, especially since I had to cover what I considered to be a minor story. I thought my writing deserved a bigger canvas. A grander tale. But I was young, ambitious and eager to please my editor.

I got to work early and reported to the desk of Mr. Clyde, the city editor of *The Examiner*. He briefed me on the assignment and informed me that the owner of Blackstone's of Beacon Hill, Jack Shepard, had been found dead earlier that morning. Jack's journal had been recovered by the authorities and handed over to our paper, which in turn Mr. Clyde handed over to me. I was also armed with a folder full of articles and photographs.

I arrived at the site by taxi late that afternoon, just as a light snow began to fall. As I made my way over the bricked sidewalk, to my amazement, and certainly most unusual for Christmas Eve, a large crowd had gathered. That was puzzling from the start.

I had done a little research but really I had very few facts in hand. Two things were certain, however: Jack Shepard was dead...and his store, Blackstone's of Beacon Hill, lay in ruins. The former was claimed by eminence above, the latter by more earthly means—eminent domain and the wrecking ball.

Chapter 2

In front of the Blackstone's lot, the silence of the descending snow was shattered by the collapse of the remaining walls and timbers and the commencement of the tumultuous battle between the wrecking ball and the store's last structure standing: the chimney. Amazingly, the crane operator had destroyed the building in what seemed like minutes, but, even after dozens of attempts, the one-ton ball could not knock the chimney down, not even a scratch, evidence of what happens when an unstoppable force meets an immovable object. Perplexed, I grabbed my pad and pen to make note of this and then began to interview the crowd.

There were locals to be sure, but many of the spectators were from out of town. When I asked them why they had assembled at Blackstone's on Christmas Eve, they answered that they were there at the invitation of Jack Shepard. They had come to receive what they called the "tenth ornament" and to hear the solution to a Christmas riddle they had all been working on.

Tenth ornament? Riddles? Jack Shepard was dead! Didn't they know? As it turned out, they had just learned about his death.

The more I spoke to people the more I came to understand. The crowd was comprised of folks from the neighborhood as well as families from all over the country who had previously visited Blackstone's as tourists. They were part of what Jack called "Blackstone's Christmas Mystery Ornament Program," which involved the purchase of 10 Christmas ornaments over the course of five years. Three ornaments were purchased the first year, two a year for the next three years, and the tenth and final ornament was to be issued on Christmas Eve at the end of the fifth year—this year. Each ornament was encoded with mysterious numbers that, when deciphered, would reveal an important message. Any of the families who correctly uncovered this message would be entered into a drawing. The lucky winner would win $2,000 in silver and gold coins.

Nine of the ornaments had already been received by the families. The revealing of the tenth and final ornament, along with the unveiling of its secret message and the drawing, would happen at midnight on Christmas Eve at the Cambridge Trust Company Bank in Boston. Of course, there were some glaring glitches in all this. Jack Shepard was dead, his store was being destroyed and, according to the bank, there was no tenth ornament!

To my bewilderment, the families were determined to stay in Boston and go to the bank at midnight anyway. Jack had obviously left a strong impression on these folks. They were shocked and saddened.

"Even though I had only met him once, he sent me the most beautiful note when my mother died," a woman from Ohio said tearfully.

"Jack was different from any person I have ever met," another traveler explained. "He had an innate sense of empathy. I was immediately at ease in his presence."

"I can't believe he's gone. When I lost work he helped me find a job. He lent me money when I knew he couldn't afford to," added a man from Georgia. "I feel a spirit such as his will surely produce an echo for all of us."

"Why are you staying and going to the bank?" I asked one man. "What do you expect to gain?"

"Listen, we're here," he said, voicing what the others were thinking. "We've traveled a long distance. We intend to see this thing to the end, if only to honor the memory of Jack and his wife, Gea. From the very first Christmas up until this one, wondrous events have been known to happen."

"Suit yourselves," I muttered to myself.

My attention was then drawn to a familiar figure standing to my right. It was Stanton Barnswell, the millionaire developer. At his side was his 12-year-old daughter, Sally. To Boston residents, Barnswell was as well known as he was disliked. By all accounts he was the meanest, greediest man in town. Barnswell's goal was to own everything on Charles Street. He planned to turn the area into a mall-like chain of stores filled with cheap imports. By charging high rents and taking a piece of the action, he could line his own pockets and those of his rich investors. Blackstone's and Jack Shepard were among his many targets...and now it was painfully clear that Barnswell had gotten what he wanted. I could sense that Mr. Barnswell was a man who wouldn't be trifled with. By the look on his face, I could tell that this developer enjoyed destroying things more than building them.

Barnswell was born into a family of wealth and privilege—a life that seemed to come with a sense of entitlement. With the destruction of Blackstone's complete, Barnswell grew ever closer to his goal of owning every business on the street, even if it meant driving out the family-owned businesses that had been around for generations. This, of course, was not his concern; only the bottom line mattered to him.

Knowing he was central to my story, I approached Barnswell for a quote and asked why he was present for the destruction.

"This is a great victory for Barnswell Enterprises," he answered defensively. "I am now the owner of this site, and something grander will take its place."

I probed further, "Was Jack Shepard a friend of yours?"

"Not really," he answered curtly. "I mean, don't get me wrong. I'm sorry he's gone, but this store could have been a gold mine in the right hands."

I responded, "In your hands, you mean?"

"Exactly," Barnswell said.

Barnswell had won for sure, but I had to wonder, at what cost? To what end? Honestly, for any one person, how much money is enough? How does one measure wealth?

The day was young, however, and before the midnight hour would strike, Barnswell would look at his life and work in a totally new light. I didn't know it then, but perhaps this change began with Sally. She had been standing at his side throughout the demolition, tears streaming down her face. I saw Barnswell's face soften as he looked at her with genuine concern. But just as quickly, his iron disposition returned, and he focused his attention back to the work in front of him.

Chapter 3

Through my research and Jack's journal entries I discovered that Jack Shepard was the only child of James and Nina Shepard, who themselves were the only children in their families. After his parents died, Jack became the last Shepard. Jack inherited Blackstone's from his father, who bought the store and building from a kindly local landlord who had retired. From the time Jack's head could peer above the top of the counter he had known no other job than his work at Blackstone's...and he loved every minute of it.

He always had a cheerful and helpful disposition, but he was not someone you'd notice in a crowded room. He seemed to be just an average guy. But when he moved, you noticed him; he had a pronounced limp and always carried a cane—the result of a childhood accident.

Apparently, at the age of 10 or so, Jack was up on the roof of the store with his father repairing shingles around the chimney when Jack lost his footing. He began to slide towards the edge of the sharply pitched roof. His father acted quickly and desperately reached for Jack's sleeve. He momentarily had ahold of him, but in the end was unable to maintain his grip. Jack tumbled four stories to the brick sidewalk below. If it hadn't been for a tree that broke his fall, Jack might not have survived at all. James Shepard never got over the guilt of being unable to prevent his son's fall. As for Jack, he never gave it another thought.

After James died, Jack kept his father's portrait in a prominent place in the store. But the store was now his, and Jack would have to place his own stamp on it. Barnswell was right about one thing: Jack was not a great businessman. Although he was beloved enough by the community and customers to keep his business afloat, he was easily distracted by other interests and pursuits, like his love of music.

You see, Jack was a very talented musician and singer. A genuine Muratore acoustic guitar was never far from his reach. Often he could be found playing songs for his customers. He loved Irish music in particular. But perhaps more of his time should have been spent managing his business.

Though he wished to be married, for years Jack's only companion was his faithful dog, Quigley. Quigley was a Welsh terrier and a valued employee. Jack had trained him to deliver packages to neighbors and customers. He seemed to know exactly where to go. Amazing! As was Jack's nature, each delivered bag of goods included an extra gift of bubble gum or an ice-cold cola as a thank-you. Although Quigley proved a great companion, it didn't compare with

the companionship of a partner in life.

This all changed when a beautiful Irish lass happened by Blackstone's one day. Her name was Gea O'Sullivan, and she was imbued with an inner beauty that made her shine. Perhaps not coincidentally, on this day, Jack made his first journal entry: *At long last, love has come.*

Gea was something else, all right. She was gorgeous and always wore a straw bonnet with multicolored ribbons upon it.

Gea had been into the shop several times before. Jack was immediately smitten with her but was too tongue-tied to say anything. However, somehow this day, he found his courage. From an upstairs window, Jack looked down at the street as Gea walked by. He grabbed his guitar and began to serenade her with an old Irish ballad, "The Galway Shawl." He sang about a "damsel" who needed no makeup or jewelry to show her beauty—just a bonnet with ribbons upon it and a Galway shawl.

It was as if the song had been written with Gea in mind. She looked up at Jack and smiled broadly. A romance began to bloom, and before long they were married. Like Jack, Gea was an orphan, and she had a heartbreaking past. I hear she was born somewhere near the Cliffs of Dooneen in Ireland. Her parents both died of typhoid fever when Gea was only four or five years old. She was moved from one orphanage to another until the age of 16, after which she became a bookkeeper for small establishments in her area. Later—and we don't know how—she found her way to America. What was unknown at the time, however, was that she was gravely ill with cancer. Beyond that, not much is known of Gea's past. What is known is that her illness and Jack's disability didn't matter a whit to either one. To most, these two were an unlikely match, but to all, a perfect fit. They both comprised the missing strengths in each other's lives.

Chapter 4

Working together, business started to pick up a bit. Gea used her bookkeeping skills and quickly organized the accounts and the inventory. Her warmth, energy and friendliness also attracted many new customers. Things seemed to be getting better. But this wouldn't last. Barnswell and his cronies had begun their campaign in earnest to own every store on Charles Street. Already, three struggling stores had been seized by eminent domain for not producing enough tax revenue for the city. Barnswell was well connected with people in high places. Barnswell knew that Jack's store was failing, and he easily made the case that he could do better. But Blackstone's would not be an easy target. Jack was a determined soul. He was going to hang on at all costs.

In order to compete, Jack and Gea had to cut back on inventory to afford the rising costs of their own quality products. Blackstone's windows and shelves became sparse. Little inventory meant fewer customers, and fewer customers meant little money coming in. Jack and Gea found it hard to make ends meet. Sometimes they were even unable to draw a salary. Only two years had passed since they joined forces, and already they worried that the future might not be as bright as they had once hoped. They feared that their efforts simply could not compete with the Barnswell machine.

Then one crisp autumn day, out of the blue, something unexpected and extraordinary happened. It was extremely windy, and fallen leaves were swirling about the brick sidewalks of Charles Street. The sun was low. Its ebbing light cast a mystical, glittering, orange glow all around. At the window, Jack marveled at this majestic beauty. Suddenly, a ragged old man seemed to burst forth from a tunnel of swirling leaves. The stranger had a long, white beard; his clothes were tattered, and he carried a large brown satchel. Jack stared in amazement, almost hypnotized. He couldn't believe his eyes. But the man was real! And he was coming right through the front door! The stranger extended his hand to Jack and introduced himself as Chester "Chimney" Colchicum.

Chapter 5

Chester "Chimney" Colchicum. Wow, what a name! Colchicum is actually the name of a flower; it's a peculiar crocus that blooms only in the fall. Chester's nickname, "Chimney," came from his trade as a mason and bricklayer, although Jack would forever call him Chester. He was an eccentric fellow, to be sure. Physically, his body seemed to sag in a world-weary sort of way. His white beard was full and unkempt. His face had a lived-in look, heavily lined and creased, yet paradoxically, his twinkling eyes were an iridescent blue. He had the large, callused hands of a hard laborer.

Chester had come to Blackstone's with a proposition. He would repair Jack's crumbling chimney in exchange for food and lodging. Blackstone's chimney had been neglected and was a fire hazard to boot. Lacking the funds for repairs, Jack couldn't resist this offer. After all, the work needed to be done, and he had plenty of old bricks laying in the rear of the store. Ever since his childhood accident, Jack had developed a fear of heights and hadn't dared to go on the roof. For Jack, this was a deal made in heaven.

Chester took up residence in the basement. Gea prepared a small corner for him near a workbench and fashioned a homey space that included a cot, lamp and small fridge. Although Chester settled in quickly, he took his own sweet time drafting his plan of operation. This was to be his masterpiece. He considered a chimney to be the heart and soul of any building. Chester's plan was simple—at least in theory. He would start at the bottom with the fireplace. Then he would work all the way up, inside the store and through three stories, until he reached the roof. The chimney on the roof was nearly five feet tall. Here he planned to cap his work with a piece of artistry that would rival any chimney ever built. Of course this meant turning the entire store upside down and disrupting everything. Chester finally got under way and took great pride in his work. To him, each new brick was as important as the last; he handled every one with the utmost care. He took his time.

Matter of fact, he seemed to take forever. One month led to another and then another. Little progress was made. Chester repaired or replaced each brick as meticulously as a master jeweler would cut a diamond. Jack was frustrated, and he wrote about it in his journal:

> *The store is in shambles. I don't understand why Chester is taking so long. Why is he seeking perfection? No one will even see his work once the walls cover everything up again.*
>
> *I asked Chester about this, and the old man had quite a reply:*

"Well, isn't that the point? Although not visible, we must work as hard on the inside as we do on the outside. It is the unseen that lasts forever. Honesty, integrity, love, mercy and forgiveness are all unseen and their mortar can sometimes weaken. But with care, faith and hard work they will stand the test of time. They'll continue to exist long after we are gone. Just as I lay these bricks, Jack, you must lay some of your own. These 'bricks' are your core and comprise your character. It is your character that will see light long after you are gone."

Chapter 6

Over the following year, the seasons came and went without much change. Chester's work still moved at a snail's pace, nowhere near completion. But the old man ate like a horse. He also had a great fondness for bubble gum, to which he helped himself at every opportunity. These things cost Jack money! Jack didn't complain, however. He seemed amused by Chester's glee over the giant bubbles he could produce.

Chester also enjoyed the social life. He made friends easily. He would spend increasingly long periods of time away from the store and could be found regaling anyone who would listen with the fantastic tales and parables he made up out of thin air.

It seemed that life was frozen in time for all. Still, flowers bloomed in the spring. The summer sun shined over simmering beaches. Autumn breezes carried colorful leaves to and fro, and snow blanketed every corner of Charles Street. It's funny, but our lives are like seasons, too. Seasons are like our souls as we are in turn hopeful, joyful, reflective and sometimes bleak.

For the Shepards, life grew increasingly difficult. Gea's health was failing, and it was obvious that radiation treatments and operations were in her future. Business had slowed to a crawl, and Barnswell maintained the pressure, bearing down on them. His constant claim that he could raise more tax revenue for the city if he took over Blackstone's seemed more and more reasonable. Jack was forced to show tax receipts repeatedly to prove that his store was a viable enterprise. Barnswell was relentless, but what rankled him more than anything was the fact that his daughter Sally had become the best of friends with Jack and Gea. Sally always hung around the store, volunteering to stock shelves, sweep floors and help Quigley deliver packages. Once, she helped Gea decorate a maypole on the old gas light in front of the store, and she became a constant presence once Gea was not able to work as much as she had before. Sally quickly became Jack's little helper and expressed on more than one occasion that she hoped to own a store like Blackstone's one day.

Even in the worst of times, Jack and Gea remained generous to those in need around them. Each Thanksgiving they would invite all those who were down on their luck or had no place to go for the holiday to their home. Over the years they paid particular attention to a woman named Etta. Etta was homeless and took up residence in an alley not far from the store. She and Jack had known each other for a long time. Etta was a very proud person and

didn't like to eat with the others. She didn't feel comfortable around anyone unless she was three sheets to the wind! Jack, therefore, always delivered her Thanksgiving meal to her alley home. At Christmas, Jack would set up a little tree for her and place a few presents—mostly food—underneath. Jack was Etta's only friend. When she would come into the store from time to time, she would pilfer things and quietly walk out. Jack would notice but simply turn the other way.

Chapter 7

No matter how much Jack and Gea gave or how hard they worked, things were spiraling downward. Concerned for his friends' well-being, Chester presented Jack and Gea with an idea that would change things dramatically: the Christmas Mystery Ornament Program. Yes, this was Chester's big idea! He said he knew "a guy way, way, way up north" who would provide the ornaments. Jack would create the secret message to be solved, and Chester would take care of the rest. Chester thought that if Jack were to offer prize money to whoever solved the riddle, more people would be inclined to join the program, and he would make his money back over time and maybe a small profit. Jack's father had left him about $2,000 in old silver and gold coins, so this would be the prize money.

Chester had made friends with the president of the Cambridge Trust Company Bank on Beacon Street. His name was Robert Athenry. Mr. Athenry had been hired as the bank's new president. Chester raved about Athenry, and on Chester's suggestion, Athenry was kind enough to make time for an after-hours meeting with Jack. Jack went to the bank with the coins and the message that he had been working on for several days. The message was in a small envelope sealed with wax. Although unorthodox, Athenry agreed to hold the secret message and ornament prize money in a special teller's vault. After hearing about the ornament program, Athenry thought it was such a great idea that he promised to be present on Christmas Eve for the arrival of the tenth ornament. And so it was. Jack, with a little apprehension, deposited the money, knowing that no matter how badly he might need it later he would never be able to touch it.

Clearly Athenry impressed Jack. Although he and Jack had only met a few times, Jack wrote extensively about him in his journal, describing him as one of the most remarkable people he knew. He felt that somehow he had met this man before. There was something so strangely familiar about the president that Jack just couldn't shake the feeling. Athenry was kind and wise and had a set of eyes that could read a person's innermost thoughts, or so it appeared. Athenry made Jack feel at ease, and while it seemed odd, even to Jack, he allowed this virtual stranger to safeguard his greatest assets.

Chapter 8

The Mystery Ornament Program eventually grew to include more than 100 families from 26 states. Over the next several years everything went like clockwork. Each Christmas Chester would disappear for a while to his basement lair and then emerge with excitement. "The ornaments are in!" he would exclaim. Jack and Gea packaged them up and shipped them out at once.

Jack was in constant contact with the families as each new ornament was produced and sent off. Jack and the families corresponded with letters regularly. In these exchanges, many of the difficulties and challenges of ordinary life were shared. Jack always had a comforting word and extended his hand whenever needed. As a result, Jack and Gea grew close with many of the families. They had grown so close, in fact, that Jack invited them all to come to Boston on Christmas Eve for the unveiling of the tenth and final ornament and riddle. Most enthusiastically accepted; they had become one big family. Jack was overjoyed at the response. It would be a Christmas in Boston to remember for all time.

Jack never knew exactly where the ornaments came from, and he never asked. But once his curiosity got the best of him. One evening, long after store hours and with Gea sound asleep upstairs, he returned home after walking Quigley. Upon entering the store, Quigley began to bark at a strange, pulsating light emanating through the floorboards from the basement. Not knowing what it might be, and worried that it may be a fire, Jack and

Quigley raced down the stairs in a panic. Rushing to Chester's quarters, they were stunned to find nothing unusual. Certainly no fire, thank God, but no strange lights either. Chester was there all right, quietly reading, his head resting on his old brown satchel. There was one broken ornament on the floor...that's all. When Jack asked Chester about these strange happenings, Chester smiled broadly and said, "Who knows? Gremlins maybe."

Though the ornaments boosted sales temporarily, Gea's health care demanded these profits. Jack was stressed, and he began to lose weight. Life was hard.

But Chester always seemed to know what to do and was ready with advice. This time, he recommended that Jack and Gea visit another man he had recently met, a Reverend named Apollo Paul. The Reverend, who hailed from Kenya, was a visiting preacher at the Park Street Church. He was charismatic, jubilant and full of conviction, and he might offer comfort to Jack and Gea's beleaguered lives. Chester believed that the Reverend's message of hope, perseverance and faith in others would resonate with the couple. Although Jack hadn't been to church in years, he was at his wits' end, so he and Gea attended the following Sunday.

Chester was right. The Reverend Apollo Paul was so dynamic that Jack was moved to write about his sermon in his journal.

The Reverend's sermon was so touching it seemed like it was written just for Gea and me. He said, "All of us need to remember what is important. Each of our lives have value, meaning and purpose. We are all a part of a long continuum — a relay team, if you will, passing along a baton of sorts. At some point we each must carry the baton for a leg of the race. The baton holds 10 things: love, kindness, faith, hope, charity, mercy, forgiveness, integrity, fidelity and empathy. If this 'baton' is not protected and passed on, the world as we know it will cease to exist. There are many faiths, philosophies and schools of thought in the world that uphold these tenets. We must love and respect them all. In so doing, there is hope for ourselves and the world."

After the service, Jack visited with the Reverend. He wanted to compliment him on his sermon and tell him that it helped him to reconcile his own thoughts, fears and doubts. Jack admitted to the Reverend that his life had grown beyond his ability to cope, and that he felt powerless to affect any change. Worse, his sadness and frustration were beginning to turn into anger.

The Reverend responded to Jack with compassion. "Why not turn a negative into a positive? Anyone can throw a brick through a window. It is *not* throwing the brick that gives us our character. Better to use the brick to build things rather than destroy them. In times of trial it is difficult not to think only of ourselves. But when we think of others our own troubles seem more manageable.

"In my own times of trial I often turn to this prayer," the Reverend said. He handed Jack a prayer card and shook his hand. "Peace be with you," he added.

Jack was speechless. He had the same bizarre feeling of familiarity about the Reverend that he did about Athenry. Jack knew he knew him from somewhere. But how could he? Yet the thought persisted. What an extraordinary person this man from afar was. Jack looked down at the prayer card:

Prayer

I asked for strength, and God
gave me difficulties to make me strong.
I asked for wisdom, and God
gave me problems to solve.
I asked for prosperity, and God
gave me brawn and brain to work.
I asked for courage, and God
gave me dangers to overcome.
I asked for love, and God
gave me troubled people to help.
I asked for favors, and God
gave me opportunities.
I received nothing I wanted.
I received everything I needed.
My prayers were answered.
—Unknown

Jack now knew for certain that the secret ornament message he had placed in the bank teller's vault was the right one. This prayer, with its wonderful, uplifting theme, and the Reverend's profound wisdom were just what Jack needed. His spirits were raised temporarily.

Chapter 9

Whether you call it fate or destiny, the future has its own way and purpose. No matter how hard we may try, we can neither predict nor affect its outcome. Like a fallen leaf in a running stream, the shore we wash up on is unknown to us. For Jack, his future and his fate would be full of challenges in the coming months.

It all began innocently enough. The fourth year of the Ornament Program was winding down. Ornaments number eight and nine again magically appeared and were shipped around the country. The final Christmas gathering and the presentation of the tenth ornament and its message were still a year away. The RSVPs for the anticipated event streamed in. And at long last Chester's chimney was beginning to take shape; it looked like he may even complete the job shortly. But the more things change the more they stay the same. Gea began to suffer painful episodes as her cancer spread, and the costs for her treatments had risen significantly. Jack's health had also deteriorated. He was still losing weight, and he had developed a severe cough. Business had come to a standstill. Barnswell was adding new businesses everywhere that stocked inexpensive imported goods that made it difficult for anyone to compete. For the first time in his life, Jack was forced to seek work beyond Blackstone's. To help make ends meet, he took an evening job at The Sevens bar, singing and playing his guitar for tips.

Meanwhile, Barnswell suffered a massive heart attack. This was a surprise to some, because most people felt he had no heart at all. He had no visitors at the hospital except for his daughter Sally and, to everyone's awe, Jack. It's hard to imagine that the man Barnswell was trying to ruin would visit him. When Jack entered the room Sally was the only one present. Even with his daughter there, Barnswell was as coarse as ever.

He asked Jack, "What are you doing here?"

Jack answered, "I wanted to see if you were all right and if I could offer help to Sally while you recover."

Barnswell didn't answer but blankly stared at the wall for a minute. Then he growled, "Give up, Shepard. You can't win."

Barnswell survived and continued to be relentless in his pursuit of Blackstone's.

But it was what followed next that shattered Jack's life forever. Gea, after years of courageously battling her disease, finally succumbed to it, dying quietly at home above Blackstone's. Jack was at her bedside when she passed away. Quigley lay quietly at her feet. Chester did all he could to console Jack, but Jack was devastated beyond measure. Hundreds of letters and flowers arrived, and there was a wonderful memorial service at the church presided over by Reverend Apollo Paul. Before Gea died, she expressed her wishes to have her ashes scattered in Ireland in the bay below the Cliffs of Dooneen. Jack would of course honor this, no matter the cost.

Heading to Ireland and closing the store for a while would use up all the resources he had left. He knew that he could not continue in life or business without Gea, and his store faced foreclosure. Barnswell had won at last. The $2,000 he had in the bank for the Ornament

Program was tempting, but he refused to touch it—his loyalty to his customers, and now friends, was too great. So Jack and Quigley went off to Ireland with Gea's remains. In a very emotional moment, with Quigley at his side, Jack scattered the ashes from the beautiful emerald green cliffs to the clear blue water below. As a final tribute, he tossed Gea's bonnet to the wind and watched as it sailed majestically outward, settling peacefully in the ocean below. He decided to keep the colorful ribbons from the bonnet and tied them to his belt. He would carry these ribbons for the rest of his life.

Upon returning home, he found that Barnswell, already alerted to his plight, had filed the necessary papers to obtain Blackstone's. He gave Jack only two weeks to move out. Even more heartlessly, he scheduled the store for demolition at the end of the year, on Christmas Eve of all days.

Ironically, Chester had just finished his work on the chimney. Every sturdy brick from the fireplace to the roof—four stories—was securely in place. Chester had completed his masterpiece. But nothing seemed to matter now. Both Jack and Chester would have to go. They spent the next two weeks packing things up for Goodwill and figuring out what to trash. Each night, with only a small candle to light the otherwise empty room, they would sit and talk into the wee hours, breaking only occasionally to take Quigley for a walk. Jack was very apprehensive about the tenth ornament. Could Chester find a way to get it to him?

"Do not worry. I will take care of it," Chester reassured.

Before they closed the door for good, Chester gave his satchel to Jack as a thank-you and remembrance of their time together. "It is my most valuable possession, and now it is yours," he said to Jack, adding, "You know, I worked awfully hard on this chimney of yours. I'm very proud of it, and I would love to show it to you before we leave."

This meant going up on the roof! Jack was not too keen on this idea, but he felt he owed Chester the final honor of inspecting his work.

Reaching the roof through a trap door was both mentally and physically challenging. His leg made the climb hard, but he was determined. When the door opened, right away Jack felt uneasy. His fear of heights was triggered by the memory of his crippling accident. He had avoided the roof all his life, and now there he was. He trembled, inching slowly along the slippery tar shingles. Chester led the way and showed no fear at all. Suddenly Chester, the great roof walker himself, slipped. He began to slide towards the edge, which was only a few feet away. Jack, petrified, like his father before him, instinctively grabbed for Chester's sleeve. He strained to hold on with every bit of strength he could muster, but it wasn't enough. Chester, released from Jack's grasp, fell four stories to the pavement. There was no tree to break his fall.

He died instantly. Oddly without fear, Jack stood at the edge of the roof looking down, and sobbed uncontrollably. Chester was gone. All hope in Jack's world seemed to vanish with him.

They say God never gives us more than we can handle in life. But, I'm not so sure. Jack lost the love of his life, his best friend and mentor, his business and home. He was forced to seek shelter in alleys like the Ettas of this world. And if that weren't enough, Christmas Eve was just around the corner. Where on God's good earth was that tenth ornament going to come from?

Chapter 10

After Chester's death, Jack stopped writing in his journal. I guess he felt there was nothing else to write about. The rest of the story is my own account, and it is a most amazing tale. Jack's promise to produce the tenth ornament and appear with Mr. Athenry at the Christmas Eve event was now by all measures seemingly impossible. He was a man of no means—destitute and utterly alone.

But a man alone with faith is never truly alone. Although I never met him, I could tell Jack had faith. I, myself, am a born skeptic. Maybe it's the reporter in me, but faith is one of those things I could never really wrap my head around. I like facts. One presupposes that just

having faith is enough to make something happen. On its face it seems preposterous—to have an unwavering belief in something with no real confirmation. Faith is funny all right. Even if you abandon faith, there is always an alternate belief. Even those who believe in "nothing" may perhaps have faith in something or some philosophy, it just wears a different mask. Surely even the most cynical among us wish and hope for something. But does that mean we have faith? I'm not so sure.

Faith or not, Jack wandered the streets, tormented, wondering how he could possibly make good on his promise to produce the tenth ornament.

Over the next months, Jack grew more ill with each passing day. He wandered aimlessly. The constant rat-a-tat-tat of his cane upon the brick sidewalks always announced his presence. Still wearing Gea's colored ribbons on his belt, he was instantly recognizable wherever he went. Quigley remained his only comfort. Jack slept in alleys and abandoned doorways. He refused all charity, even from those whom he had so generously helped in the past. Why? Who knows? He seemed to want to make his own way no matter what, though he did accept some help from Etta. Her daily rounds of begging and pilfering were sometimes Jack's only source of food and clothing. His sole possessions were his Muratore guitar and Chester's satchel, which he used as a pillow at night and where he stored what little he had.

On occasion Jack would play his guitar at The Sevens in exchange for meals for himself and Etta and scraps for Quigley. He always played the same four Irish ballads. "The Garden Song"…you know the little ditty, "inch by inch, row by row, someone bless these seeds I sow." The songs "Galway Shawl" and "The Cliffs of Dooneen" were always sung for Gea. Finally, the tune "Town I Loved So Well" was probably a lament to what had been lost on Charles Street. The song recounts the story of a man who returns to his war-torn childhood hometown, only to find it destroyed. By anyone's standards Charles Street's former self was unrecognizable. Barnswell had managed to make the business district like any other, destroying its unique character and appeal and driving out generations of family-owned businesses. Barnswell's investors were thrilled…all six of them! How do six greedy investors interested only in money trump an entire community? It must have been painful for Jack to walk past Blackstone's, all withered and boarded up and waiting for the Christmas Eve wrecking ball.

Chapter 11

Well, Christmas Eve came. The day began with Jack's death. He was found face down in a snowbank. Quigley lay on top of him whimpering uncontrollably. He had apparently died from exposure. Most agreed that Jack's death signaled the final nail in the coffin in the death of a community. He had been one of the lone voices in the struggle against Barnswell's crusade. But some things in life and death are not what they seem. In fact, Jack's death was not an ending, but a beginning. On this night before Christmas, all that was and all that would be converged at the crossroads of extraordinary events. Events that boggled the mind, transformed a community, its inhabitants and even me. I was slowly being drawn into something I couldn't comprehend. Something surreal.

On this strange occasion, the past, the present and the future somehow found one another, setting off a whirlwind of wonder that was full of the unexplained. As dawn breaks on any given

day, we move on with our lives expecting nothing out of the ordinary. But at any moment of any day, we can bear witnesses to an extraordinary human drama that leads us to question its purpose. We may not have designed the moment, but was the moment designed for us? I didn't know it at the time, but before the day was through, my moment would come.

And so it was on that snowy Christmas Eve day. All the players in this particular human drama, mostly unknown to each other, were going about their routines. At the Boston Park Plaza Hotel, the so-called ornament families were preparing to head over to Blackstone's. In Chelsea, a crane operator was attaching a wrecking ball to his machine. In Beacon Hill, Barnswell was signing the final contracts for the destruction of Blackstone's. Sally sat in his office begging him to stop and to preserve the store instead. Over at The Sevens, the staff readied the bar for business, stocking beer and setting up a Christmas tree. Etta began her morning in search of Jack, who had not returned the night before, as was his habit. Soon the paths of these individuals would cross for an unforgettable night.

As for me, after meeting with Mr. Clyde and doing a little preliminary research, I grabbed a cup of coffee, called Conti's Cab and headed for Charles Street, which brings us to where I started this story: at the scene of the destruction of Blackstone's.

After the families dispersed, I couldn't help thinking how futile it was for them to stay. Why didn't they just go home? What did they think could be accomplished by keeping their midnight appointment at the bank? At the time, I thought, how sad, how blind, how foolhardy.

Anyway, after the crowd left, only Barnswell and the crane operator remained. The operator was mystified as to why it was physically impossible to knock the chimney down. After all, he had done this successfully many times before.

"Not to worry," said Barnswell emphatically. "We'll dynamite it tomorrow."

The snow was falling heavier now, and with everyone gone, I walked amongst the rubble, took a few pictures, made a few more notes and then wandered over to that invincible chimney. There it stood, against all odds, the lone sentinel, witness and judge to all before it. Absolutely amazing! I sifted through the ashes of the fireplace and found two things: a Morgan silver dollar and a piece of bubble gum. I knew from Jack's journal that the bubble gum was surely Mr. Chester "Chimney" Colchicum's. He was rarely seen without a mouthful and was always blowing bubbles. The silver dollar was probably Jack's and meant to be part of the bank's prize money. Poor fella, I thought to myself. It was probably his last buck. I slipped it into my pocket—you know, for good luck or something. I still have it.

Chapter 12

It was growing dark. My work was mostly done at the site, so I headed over to The Sevens to have a few. There I'd look over the folder again and perhaps interview some of the locals about Jack's untimely death. From out of a now near blizzard I entered the bar, which was loud, smoky and boisterous. It was packed to the rafters with people. To my good fortune, I found myself in the midst of a makeshift memorial for Jack. Beers were on the house. Barely heard over the din, a guitarist was playing Jack's favorite Irish tunes. Locals, standing on chairs and tables, took turns making speeches and toasting the memory of Jack Shepard. The testimonials were amazing. Jack had certainly touched a lot of lives—each anecdote was more emotional than the last. Apparently, no one had been exempt from Jack's kindness and generosity. As I fingered Jack's silver dollar in my pocket I was reminded of two old adages: "you can't take it with you" and "the only thing you can take with you is that which you have given away." Jack had clearly given much.

I found a spot at the end of the bar and settled in. Two beers appeared instantly.

"Here's to Jack," someone exclaimed, clinking my glass.

I took a huge sip of my beer and leafed through some of the photos and articles in my folder. It was interesting to see *The Examiner*'s archival pictures and articles about Jack and Gea and the host of characters that filled their lives. The pictures of Chester (bubblegum bubbles included!), the Reverend Apollo Paul and bank president Robert Athenry were the most captivating. It was interesting for me to put faces to the names. Jack had written so much about these gentlemen in his journal. Each had a face full of character; lined and with a worldly-wise look about them. All three possessed knowing twinkles in their eyes. They all looked trustworthy. I could see why Jack held them in such high esteem. I, too, felt as if I knew them just by seeing their pictures. Strange.

I was jarred from my contemplation by a hearty slap on the back that sent my beer into my lap. I turned around to see an old woman: Etta! She had Quigley with her. Etta knew I was a reporter. She had seen me at Blackstone's earlier. She was full of emotion, perhaps a little hysterical, and tears streamed down her face. She claimed she had a story for me. Incredibly, she had seen Jack die.

Now this may sound a little fantastic, especially since it came from an excitable woman who was quaffing every pint of ale within reach, but this is what she told me: The night before,

Jack had left for a walk, but he had never returned. Concerned, Etta searched for him at first light. She finally caught a glimpse of him near the corner of Charles and Beacon. She was about 75 yards away. He was clearly visible. The predicted snowfall for the day had not yet begun, although it was quite windy. As she approached, she noticed a sudden swirling of dead leaves, almost tunnel-like, rise before Jack. He walked right into the vortex, disappeared momentarily, and emerged on the other side. Then he collapsed. Just as he hit the ground (now bear with me on this one), the satchel he always carried—Chester's satchel—began to rattle and roll. It opened on its own and sent forth an explosion of thick beams of lights and colored orbs into the sky.

Do you believe it? I've got to tell you, I thought Etta was spinning one heck of a tall tale.

She then added, to my surprise, "Are you going to be at the bank at midnight?"

I said I would. What the heck? I thought. I had come this far on this bizarre journey; I might as well go all the way.

As I got up from my barstool, Etta said, "Jack will be there, you know."

"What are you talking about?" I shot back. "What makes you think so?"

"Because he told me so, you dang fool," she sputtered. "And I believe him! Now hoist me up on the bar, Sonny Boy!"

So I did, and I lifted Quigley up to the bar too, for good measure.

Standing on the bar, she yelled to the drunken crowd before her, "You all know my story. On account of what I seen, I'm goin' to the bank at midnight. Them families at the Plaza come from all over to see Jack, and they're goin'! What about you? Are you all gonna let them go by themselves? Who believes in Jack more than us? Who's with me?"

A crescendo of cheers filled the room. "We're with you, Etta! Let's all go!"

Then someone piped in, "Yeah, and let's grab that bum Barnswell on the way and take him with us, whether he likes it or not!" The room immediately filled with boos and catcalls.

It was growing to a fever pitch. Time for me to leave. As I pushed my way through the throng, a young man tapped me on the shoulder. He had something to tell me.

"You know, I seen that light as well. A bunch of us did," he said softly.

Chapter 13

Outside, the storm raged on, nearly whiteout conditions. I made my way to Toscano's Restaurant to grab a bite to eat. It was packed. Like The Sevens, the room was abuzz with debate over Jack and the approaching midnight hour. Etta's story had spread fast. As I made my way to my table, I eavesdropped on the conversations around me.

"Are you going to believe the ravings of an old homeless woman?" a disbelieving husband goaded his wife.

"Oh, come on, dear," she replied impatiently. "It's for Jack. It won't hurt to take a look. Who knows what we'll find? After all, it's Christmas!" Then she paused and turned to a table behind her. "Right, Mr. Barnswell?"

Barnswell? Would you believe he was seated at a rear table with Sally? His head was down. Once the woman brought attention to him, others chimed in.

"Yeah, what about it, Barnswell? Don't you believe in the spirit of Christmas?" The room erupted with laughter.

Barnswell stood up and indignantly threw his napkin down on his table. "Christmas is just for fools. It's just another holiday, for cryin' out loud. Simply a day off." He then stormed out, pulling Sally by the hand.

This community had certainly come alive! What a crazy evening it was turning out to be.

Toscano's was situated directly across the street from the Blackstone's, and I was able to secure a nice window seat. I gazed through the snow squall across the street at the now-empty lot and that indomitable chimney. What kind of story was I going to submit to my editor? The story had not unfolded as simply as I expected. Sure, the basics were there: the who, what, why and where…a deceased owner, a destroyed building, a greedy developer and Charles Street on Beacon Hill. I had enough elements to submit a story. Facts are facts. But even though I was not usually prone to fantasy or science fiction, all of the unanswered questions kept spinning

in my head. Like that chimney across the street, tunnels of swirling leaves, light beams and orbs shooting toward the sky, those resolute and determined ornament families and a cast of characters directly out of Central Casting.

My thoughts were all over the place. I thought about Etta, the poorest of the poor. She had been given the least in life, but her faith was great. And then there was Barnswell, who had everything and believed in nothing. And those swirling leaves—they were oddly reminiscent.

I flipped back through Jack's journal, and there they were. Chester had first appeared in front of Blackstone's out of a tunnel of swirling leaves. Jack had disappeared into a tunnel of swirling leaves before he died. How was that possible?

I scribbled down a few notes, but the hour was getting late. It was a little after 11 o'clock. I paid my tab and headed over to the Boston Park Plaza Hotel to mingle with the ornament families.

It was a tough slog getting over there in the blinding snow. When I arrived, many people had already assembled out front, preparing to leave for the bank. Some were writing down their guesses for what the secret message might be. Their answers would've been entered into a raffle had Jack still been around. Why on Earth were they still doing this, I wondered?

"What's the harm?" one person asked, as if reading my mind. "We've decided to see this contest to the end as if Jack was still with us."

Spirits were high and hopeful. I couldn't help thinking, hopeful for what? They knew Jack was dead; there would be no ornaments, no raffle and no prize money.

Chapter 14

In moments, more than a hundred people had gathered. Someone passed out song sheets, and off went the throng, into the storm, winding through the Boston Public Garden toward the bank singing "O Come All Ye Faithful." What a spectacle!

I thought of the disappointment the crowd would surely face once they arrived at the bank on the other side of the garden to...nothing. I was there to cover a story, but I couldn't bear to watch that. No way would I follow them on a fool's errand. Better to get to the bank after the fact and grab an unfortunate few for comments.

Meanwhile, the inebriated mob at The Sevens had cleared out of the bar and marched up Charles Street, over to Chestnut Street, where they created a ruckus in front of Barnswell's house. Well, when ol' Barnswell came out of the house to drive the invaders off of his lawn, the crowd grabbed him, picked him up on their shoulders and carried him toward the bank. Barnswell kicked and yelled profanities the whole way. Sally followed the mob, secretly happy, because her father had forbidden her to go on her own.

Unaware of all of this, I killed a little time by taking a roundabout way to the bank, toward the Park Street Church, up Park Street to the State House and then down Beacon. I wanted a chance to clear the cobwebs from my head and try again to make sense of all this. I arrived in front of the church just as the first of its 12 midnight bells tolled. I was startled, first by the sound of the bells, then I went back on my heels when I saw a man suddenly in front of me. My God, that's Athenry! I recognized him from the photos.

He looked at me for a moment, smiled and said, "Merry Christmas," calling me by name.

I made no reply. I was speechless. My goodness, how could he have known my name? And how strange to see him here. He must have been heading to the bank too.

Just as quickly as he appeared, Athenry vanished into the swirling snows and headed up Park Street toward the State House. I stood there half paralyzed for a moment, then hurried after him.

"Mr. Athenry, wait a moment!" I called out. There was no reply. When I got to the corner of Beacon and Park, Athenry was nowhere to be seen. How could he have disappeared so quickly?

I was trying to catch my breath when my eyes focused on a figure emerging from under

the glow of an old gas streetlight in front of the State House. I expected Athenry, but from behind the pole, I saw a bubblegum bubble grow, behind which was a tall, white-bearded man. Goodness gracious! It wasn't Athenry, it was Chester "Chimney" Colchicum himself! The thick snow made it hard to see, but I was sure of it. Yes, it was Chester! I recognized him from the photographs I had just looked over. He gave me a slight nod and a wink and then moved rapidly down Beacon Street toward the bank.

I tried to keep up. I ran, slipping and sliding, down the west side of the street. Chester

was on the east side. A few passing cars prevented me from crossing over. At the corner of Walnut and Beacon, I caught a glimpse of Chester passing under another street lamp. But when I looked again, I realized that it wasn't him…it was the Reverend Apollo Paul. And he was blowing a bubblegum bubble! This was just crazy! I've got to be dreaming, I thought. Were the three…one? My adrenaline was really flowing now; my heart felt like it was going to pop out of my chest, and my head was spinning. Maybe my mind was playing tricks on me.

Chapter 15

Everything was happening too quickly. So quickly, in fact, that I felt like I was in some sort of altered state. I simply couldn't comprehend what I was seeing. From that point, I don't even remember how I arrived in front of the bank, but all of sudden there I was. The ornament families—a hundred or more people—were outside the bank window. They had been joined by the denizens of The Sevens and their prize captive, Barnswell.

The crowd was pointing, cheering and chattering wildly at what they were seeing inside. What could it be? I squeezed through the mob to take a look. Next to me stood Barnswell, Sally, Etta and Quigley, who was barking excitedly.

Etta looked at me, then to Barnswell and then to the mass behind her. She yelled, "I told ya he'd come."

I almost didn't want to look up, but I did. There, before all of us, were Jack and Gea! My jaw dropped. Barnswell's eyes widened, and he gasped noticeably. Sally beamed with joy. A huge roar erupted from the crowd. At first glance Jack and Gea seemed to be in the flesh, but then, amazingly, their bodies started to turn translucent. They flickered a bit and then—poof!—they disappeared from view. They had completely vanished.

There was a stunned silence among the horde, broken by a loud *POP!* We all turned to our right, and there was Athenry, bursting a bubblegum bubble and removing the gum from his lips.

With great cheer, Athenry shouted, "Merry Christmas, everyone! For those who don't know me, I am Robert Athenry, president of the bank."

We hoped he might offer some explanation for what we witnessed, but instead, he continued, "I'm sorry to hear that your great friend Jack passed away today; you have my deepest sympathies. However, I promised him I would be here tonight to open the vault, so here I am."

"Yeah, but he was just here with Gea in your bank!" someone yelled.

"That couldn't be, I'm the only one with the keys," Athenry responded, jangling some keys. "But let's go inside and take a look." He unlocked the door. Quigley was the first in, followed by Barnswell, Sally, Etta and me, and the others. As we entered, we scanned the room for evidence of Jack and Gea. There was none. The crowd peppered Athenry with questions. He could only offer that maybe we had imagined Jack to be there, because we had all wanted to see him so badly.

But what about me? I saw them too, and I didn't know Jack from Adam.

The crowd quieted a bit, perhaps questioning their vision. Athenry proceeded with the

business at hand. He asked the ornament families to hand him their solutions to the riddle, and placed them in a jar. He then went over to the vault and started to turn the tumbler. The families, of course, couldn't be sure that anything would be in the vault.

Athenry turned the tumbler right, left and right again, opening the huge door to the vault. A gasp sounded from the crowd. There it was: a sack of silver and gold coins, a sealed envelope with the final riddle enclosed and hundreds of those number 10 ornaments. Jack had kept his promise; the last Shepard had come through after all.

Athenry pulled out one of the solutions to the riddle from the raffle and announced that a family from Wyoming, the Quintanas, was the winning family. A cheer of congratulations erupted as Athenry passed out the ornaments one by one.

Chapter 16

After reveling in the awe of the moment, everyone slowly dispersed, though some were still shaking their heads at what they had just experienced. I hung behind along with Athenry, Barnswell, Sally and Etta. Quigley continued to sniff around the bank, growing frenzied in the corner of the vault. What he found left all of us speechless yet again. He had discovered Jack's cane and Gea's bonnet with all the ribbons on it. This, upon everything else, was just too much to comprehend.

Etta handed the cane and bonnet to Sally. "I think Jack and Gea would've wanted you to have these. And someone's going to have to watch over Quigley, too. Will you do that for me, Sally?"

Sally was overjoyed to say the least. Throughout this extraordinary chain of events, Barnswell had not said a word. Even he didn't know what to make of what he had experienced. Without a peep, he took Sally's hand and left, with Quigley in tow.

I walked Etta to the door and thanked her for everything, then I waited outside for Athenry to close up. I had many questions for him. But you know what? He never came out. As a matter of fact, when I went in to check on him, the bank was completely empty. He had disappeared just as mysteriously as Jack and Gea had. He was never to be heard from again. In fact, save for the Beacon Hill community and the ornament families, he was virtually unknown. The same was true for Chester and Apollo Paul. It was as if they never existed—known only in hearts, hopes and souls. To those who believed in them, they were real. To those who didn't, they were merely fiction.

Chapter 17

Over the course of the years following that extraordinary Christmas Eve, many profound and wonderful things occurred.

The ornament families returned home. Strangely, much of what they had experienced they kept to themselves. It was considered a private matter and so intensely personal that they would only share it with loved ones.

Barnswell had the biggest change of heart of all. He rebuilt Blackstone's to its original specifications around that stubborn old chimney. He also returned many of the other stores to their original owners free of charge.

Etta was enrolled in a sparkling new home for the aged, built by none other than Barnswell.

Sally grew up, got married and had six children. She is currently the owner of Blackstone's.

Quigley passed on, but he left a puppy that Sally named Quigley II.

Yep, the old neighborhood had come back in a glorious way!

As for me, that night I was in a daze. The storm had abated somewhat, so I turned up my collar and headed home. As Martin Buber once wrote in the 1600s, "All journeys have secret destinations of which the traveler is unaware." On my long journey home through the deserted streets of Boston, I felt more alone than ever in the corridors of my mind. I tried hard to absorb what I had just experienced. What sort of story would I submit to my editor? I decided to play it safe and just stick to the "facts" of the day. After all, if I told the real story, I might have been fired; I had more questions than answers. This experience upended my entire belief system on every level. I no longer knew what I believed.

In journalism school, I was taught to report only the facts, to resist the urge to give my own opinions. I was encouraged to question and cast doubt upon everything to such a degree that it had clouded my own convictions. I mean, I used to believe in Christmas, peace on earth, goodwill towards men—all that stuff. When did I stop believing or expressing myself?

Now some of those old feelings bubbled to the surface. As I got closer to home, I grew more certain that what I had experienced was miraculous. Maybe I shouldn't play it safe—I should tell the truth, though it would be hard for others to swallow. Whether they were apparitions, ghosts or angels didn't matter; I had seen them. I had scoffed at faith, yet I had seen faith rewarded. I had no idea why Chester's chimney did not fall; but it became a symbol in my mind of unshakable faith. Where did Chester get the ornaments? Did the tenth ornaments